Title: Be a Millionaire of Kindness
Website: www.billionaireofkindness.com
Publisher: Hamilton Enterprises, Denver Colorado
Date Published: August 4, 2015
Copyrighted: August 4, 2015©
Author: Dr. Peter Zrinscak D.C.
Contributor: David G. Hamilton, MBA
ISBN: 978-0988769496
Printed by Create Space Publishing, a subsidiary or Amazon

Be a Millionaire of Kindness

Be a Millionaire of Kindness

15 Things that you can
"Do and Say"
that will help you to become
"Filthy Rich" with Kindness!

By Dr. Peter T. Zrinscak D.C.
Contributions made by David
Hamilton, MBA

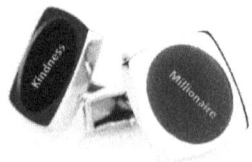

A Few Very Important Words....

Hello. My name is Peter and thank you for reading my book.

This is a book of "techniques" of things to "do and say" that can help you express kindness to other people. My intention is that the person using these "techniques" will do so with a genuine and honest heart, without intentions of manipulation or receiving something in return. This was not written to be a lesson in language but to "get-you-thinking" about common phrases that are used every day that may or may not have unintended consequences.

I am a self-declared Millionaire of Kindness! I just seem to have a knack for being kind to others, even when others are not being very kind to me.

The 15 Principles of Kindness in this book have helped me develop deep, lasting relationships and friendships and have given me a reason to live life to the fullest. I live to help others around me to feel good and to be the best they can.

These ideas have brought more kindness to my little circle of life and when you spend, spend and spend your Kindness, you will bring more kindness to your circle of life and your influence will have a lasting effect on others. Eventually, I hope all of our little circles will overlap and we can all be kinder to each other.

Thank you for picking up my book. Please be as kind to all those you come in contact with, and remember that the eye can't always see what sorrow exists in other people's lives. Be as kind as you can to everyone that you can! Do this and watch how you become richer and wealthier ... a Millionaire of Kindness!

God Bless!

Table of Contents

The 15 Things that Millionaires of Kindness "Do and Say" that make them Millionaires.

1. Millionaires rarely, if ever, use the words "But, However & Yet".

2. Millionaires are cautious when using "All or Nothing" words. Instead, they use lots of "In Between" words.

3. Millionaires say "You're Welcome" when someone says "Thank You".

4. Millionaires say: "Please", "Thank you" and "Excuse Me /Pardon Me" on a very regular basis.

5. Millionaires ask lots of questions and extend invitations. They give very little advice...rather they offer support.

6. Millionaires say "I'm sorry I hurt you" when they offend or hurt someone.

7. Millionaires tell others that they are Right when they are right, and sometimes even when they aren't right.

8. Millionaires tell others they are Wrong when they are wrong, and sometimes even when they aren't wrong.

9. Millionaires say "It hurts me when you (do something that hurt me)."

10. Millionaires listen to others deeply and

intently, without interruption. They also let others cry without interruption.

11. Millionaires make Eye Contact with others.

12. Millionaires Smile on a regular basis.

13. Millionaires give Complements to others all day long.

14. Millionaires receive Compliments with acceptance and gratitude.

15. Millionaires tell others that they are Proud of them on a regular basis.

The 15 Things that Millionaires of Kindness Do and Say that make them Millionaires.

Millionaires rarely, if ever, use the words "But, However & Yet"

Millionaires of Kindness understand that the words "<u>but</u>, <u>however</u> & <u>yet</u>" are usually used, and often unknowingly, in very hurtful ways. "<u>But</u>, <u>however</u> & <u>yet</u>" are negating and interrupting words. They interrupt the sentence and negate what was said previously. The most commonly used of these three words is "<u>but</u>".

Have you noticed how "<u>but</u>, <u>however</u> and <u>yet</u>" are usually used in a way that pretty much says:

"I heard what you are saying <u>but</u> my way is the right way"?

It doesn't matter if it is "but", "however" or "yet" that is being used. These words are used to say the last part of the sentence is right, and the first part is wrong.

In other words, you are wrong and I am right.

Using "<u>but</u>, <u>however</u> and <u>yet</u>" can really be a form of verbal bullying. The person using these words negates what other people are saying in the conversation. They are saying that your ideas don't have value and you are wrong. This is rude and not acceptable. This is a very unkind way to speak to others.

Pay attention to a variety of people speak and you will probably notice that many people use "but, however and yet" in a way that negates others. Unfortunately, there are people with influential positions in Government, on TV, on Radio, in Higher Education and in Positions of Authority that do this. Perhaps some do this knowingly to gain power over others and some do it unknowingly. Perhaps they have learned that they can get their way for the moment, by negating and bullying other people.

Millionaires of Kindness do not say these words. They are very aware and cautious with using their "buts, howevers and yets". They catch themselves and "bite their tongue" if they are about to, or tempted to use these words. If, by accident, a Millionaire says "but", they will catch themselves, retract the "but" and apologize. Then they will reconstruct their sentence in a way that does not include the "but".

Here are examples of a common sentences that use "but, however and yet" in a negating way:

    1. "You are doing a good job but there is room for some improvement".

    2. "I liked your plan, however, we are going to continue with the original plan".

    3. "You are doing much better yet you still aren't ready for the starting position".

Let's analyze the first example that uses the word "but". This sentence can be broken down into 3 parts:

    1. You are doing a good job

2. But

3. There is room for some improvement.

The first part is a nice complement. The second part is the interruption. The third part is a statement of advice, which can often be critical.

The person receiving this sentence receives a complement, has the compliment interrupted and then gets advice about something they aren't doing very well, all in a matter of a few seconds.

Here are three ways to remedy the above sentence:

1. Remove the "but" and make two sentences.

2. Replace the "but" with an "and".

3. Say only one of the two sentences. Save the other for another time.

This now becomes:

1.   You are doing a good job. There is room for some improvement.

2. You are doing a good job and there is room for some improvement.

3. You are doing a good job. (Save "There is room for   some   improvement"   for   another time.)

4.   There is room for some improvement. (Save "You are doing a good job" for   another time.)

Millionaires will usually choose #3 or #4 and separate this into two sentences and save the other part for another time. Millionaires know that the basic formula of a sentence using "<u>but</u>" is to negate something said previous to it.

Millionaires, being the efficient people that they are, ask: "What is the purpose of saying <u>but</u>"? The Millionaire's answer is that there is not a purpose in saying something and then negating it. There is no need to say "but" in the first place!

Millionaires prefer to separate complements from advice and critiques. They know that people are sensitive and it is hurtful to be elated with a compliment and then within a few seconds, be told of something that they are not doing as well as expected.

Millionaires of Kindness rarely say "<u>but,</u> <u>however</u> and <u>yet</u>" to other people because they are disrespectful and hurtful words. When Millionaires catch themselves saying these words they will stop and rephrase their wording and apologize if necessary. When in a discussion of conflicting ideas, Millionaires use the word "and" a lot and will separate opposing ideas into separate sentences to avoid hurting or disrespecting other people.

Millionaires are cautious when using "All or Nothing" words. Instead, they use lots of "In Between" words

Millionaires of Kindness strive to be very accurate in putting their observations of life into words. They are aware that there is a tendency to describe life in "all or nothing" terms in their own thoughts and in their words when speaking to other people. Millionaires resist this tendency because they understand that doing so severely limits and hurts their life and also other people. "All or nothing" words are "extreme" words.

The "all" part of "all or nothing" are words such as <u>every</u>, <u>always</u>, <u>all</u> etc. Millionaires understand that when they do say "all", they make a commitment and they really mean "all".

The same is true for the "nothing" part of "all or nothing". These are words such as <u>never, no one, nothing</u> etc. Millionaires understand that when they say "nothing", they make a commitment and they really mean "nothing".

Millionaires observe that many people are very careless when using "all or nothing" words. For example, have you heard anyone, or perhaps yourself, say something such as:

I <u>always</u> end up doing <u>all</u> the work. (100% of time)

It <u>never</u> works out for me. (0% of time)

<u>No one</u> really cares <u>anymore</u>. (0%, 100% of time)

<u>All</u> people are really mean. (100% of people)

<u>All</u> (people of a certain race) are bad. (100% of people)

<u>Nothing</u> good ever happens to me. (0% of the time)

<u>Every time</u> I try to do "good" something "bad" happens. (100% of the time)

You can't trust <u>anyone</u> these days. (100% of people)

Really? You *always* end up doing *all* the work? Come on...*always*? *All* the time? Or just "some" of the time? Or more often than you should? *All* people are bad? Really? And you are such an expert to say that *all* people of a certain race, gender or creed are bad? It can actually seem kind of silly to see human thought broken down to its basics like this.

Millionaires recognize that most statements using "all or

nothing" words are inaccurate. These extreme words are damaging because if you repeat them enough, you will begin to believe them. Yes, you shouldn't say them...yes you should "think more positive". The reality is, you could just be <u>more accurate</u>.

Most of the time, people start using these words because they are frustrated. They have been hurt and they don't want to admit they are hurt, and they don't want to be disappointed in the future. They start repeating "extreme" words, associating them with a few past experiences. The scary thing is they start believing what they are saying and imposing that viewpoint on "many other places", including other people.

Millionaires also understand that prejudice begins with the use of "all or nothing" words. For example:

> <u>(All people)</u> of a certain race, are bad people.

When it is stated this simply and clearly, Millionaires see how easy it is for prejudice to begin in the mind. Millionaires also see how easy it is to stop prejudice in the mind. It simply comes down to wording. That's why Millionaires are careful using "all or nothing words". They use lots of "in between" words, rather than "all or nothing" words.

Below is a full spectrum list of descriptive words from 0% to 100%. The 100% is the "all" and the 0% is the "nothing". Then there are some of the "in-between" words and their general definitions and ranges:

All (Always, Every etc.)	100%
Most	80% to 99%
Often	60% to 80%
Half	50%
A Lot	50% to 70%
Many	40% to 80%
Some	20% to 49%
Occasionally	5% to 20%
Rarely	1% to 5%
Nothing (Never, Nobody, etc.)	0%

This chart is a guideline and is certainly up for interpretation. Millionaires understand others may feel that the percentages are a little bit different for their personal use. Although there will be variations within these definitions, most people relate to these estimations. Their chart may be a little different, and they might not assign the exact same percentages as in this chart. They will vary from person to person and also with the situation or events that people are describing.

Here are some examples of using the "in-between" words:

Some people are really crazy in this world. (20% - 49%)

Occasionally someone really gets me angry. (5% - 20%)

Most of the time I'm pretty happy   (80% - 99%)

On a rare occasion I think I'm going crazy with anger. (1% - 5%)

I feel like the world is good most of the time.   (80% - 99%)

The spirit of these definitions is to be accurate when describing thoughts, things and events in life. This isn't to say that you shouldn't use all or nothing words to describe life. Millionaires sometimes use all or nothing words. They are just very careful. Here are some beneficial examples of using "all or nothing":

I will never take my anger out on another person. (0%)

I will never be inappropriate with a child.   (0%)

I will do my best to be honest all the time. (100%)

I will always be kind to other people. (100%)

Millionaires are aware of the power of "all or nothing" words and "in between" words. Millionaires strive to be as accurate as possible with their words and choose their words accurately and honestly as close to 100% of the time as they can. Millionaires strive to do their best and sometimes they do make errors or mistakes.

Millionaires do their best to take responsibility when they make a mistake and they apologize when they do. The great thing about "in-between" words is that it is a vocabulary that allows for success and excellence. They are constructive words because they are accurate and true. Millionaires take advantage of these words to accurately describe the world around them and also their inner feelings.

Millionaires of Kindness know that the words they say and think are, in a big part, what make them Millionaires. They choose their words in life very carefully. Millionaires are especially careful of using "all or nothing" words, as they can lock a person into unhealthy and destructive commitments. Millionaires sometimes realize that they use an inaccurate word and they stop using it and replace it with a more accurate "in-between" word. This is constructive and accurate thinking and speaking.

Millionaires say "You're Welcome" when someone says "Thank You"

Millionaires of Kindness recognize that when a person says "Thank You" to them, it is an act of appreciation directed towards them. Millionaires acknowledge this "thank you" in a kind and respectful way.

Millionaires are careful and deliberate with their responses to a "thank you". They know that a person who has extended appreciation, in the form of a "thank you", has given them an opportunity to accept the "thank you". Millionaires love these kinds of opportunities and they try their darnedest to express themselves with elegance and style.

Unfortunately, much too often, Millionaires observe many other people responding to a "Thank you" with a response such as:

1. No problem.

2. Oh hey, it was nothing.

3. No...Thank you.

4. No worries

5. No biggie.

6. Don't mention it

While these responses could be very well intentioned, they may not be fully representing the gratitude of the person being thanked. These responses could be consciously or sub-consciously interpreted as ungrateful responses. Millionaires make sure this doesn't happen to them and they make sure that their responses are interpreted as kind and grateful.

Millionaires like to stop everything that is going on around them and put 100% of their focus on the person who is thanking them. Millionaires make sure that the person feels special, at least for a couple of seconds. They may even make gentle, respectful physical contact to get their full attention. Millionaires will look into their eyes, smile and have a humble, non-threatening body position.

Then, Millionaires will genuinely say "you're welcome". The "you're welcome" may be accompanied by other words such as:

1. "Wow, that makes me feel good...you're so welcome"

2. "Oh my gosh, that is so kind of you, I really appreciate your thank you"

3. "That's so sweet of you to say that... you're so very welcome"

Millionaires have many variants of the "you're welcome" that suit their individualities. Millionaires are self-expressive and it keeps life fresh and exciting. They avoid having a standard response to the same question or phrase. Millionaires are certainly known for their flair and creativity, so you will rarely observe a Millionaire repeat a comment or response. When they do say phrases regularly, they put a unique and special emotion into each phrase for the person they are saying it to.

Many Millionaires compare a "thank you" to an "offering of a handshake". When offered a handshake, Millionaires reach out and shake the other persons hand. A refusal to shake a person's hand is usually interpreted as rejection, disrespect or that one feels that they are "too good" for them.

Millionaires have it in their mind that not responding to a thank you with a "you're welcome" with humbleness, a smile and eye contact would be comparative to refusing to shake a person's hand that was offered to them.

Millionaires genuinely say "you're welcome" when offered a "thank you". It is very simple, and perhaps because of its simplicity, saying "you're welcome" is a response that is sometimes overlooked. They know this is an excellent place to connect with others and to build respectful, constructive and healthy relationships.

Millionaires of Kindness love to extend kindness when someone thanks them. They stop time and make a special moment for another person in just a few short seconds. Millionaires love to make other people feel special for the seemingly small things in life. When a Millionaire is thanked for something, they look into other persons eyes, make physical contact when appropriate, smile, and say "You're welcome". Millionaires will usually include some extra words of appreciation. Each "You're Welcome" is sincere and unique.

Millionaires say: "Please", "Thank you" and "Excuse Me /Pardon Me" often

Millionaires of Kindness are kind and courteous people. There seems to be no limit to the kind things that Millionaires will do and say. Millionaires definitely say their "pleases, thank yous and excuse mes" many times throughout the day!

Millionaires say "please" when they ask for something, say "thank you" when they receive something and they say "excuse me" or "pardon me" when they interrupt someone.

Please's

Millionaires say "please" when they ask for something. It can happen many times throughout the day. It could be for very simple requests. The general rule is that anytime that a Millionaire asks for something, they add a "please". It is also important to be very specific in what you are asking for. Examples are:

"Could you <u>please</u> pass the salt?"

"I would appreciate it if you would <u>please</u> quiet down."

"Could you <u>please</u> stop saying that, it hurts my feelings."

Thank You's

Millionaires say "thank you" when they receive something. It could be a something delivered on a request or something given to then without asking. The general rule is that anytime a Millionaire receives something, they add a "thank you".

"<u>Thank you</u> for sharing your feelings with me."

"I cant <u>thank you</u> enough for taking me to the store"

"<u>Thank you</u> for helping me over the last year"

Excuse Me's

Millionaires say "excuse me" or "pardon me" when they bump into someone, when they want to get someone's attention, or when they want to join into a conversation. Anytime a Millionaire feels that they have interrupted someone, whether it is with a stranger or someone they know, they are saying "excuse me" or "pardon me".

"<u>Pardon me</u>, could you help me with this?"

"<u>Excuse me</u>, I didn't mean to bump into you."

"Oh I'm sorry, <u>please</u> <u>excuse me</u>."

Millionaires literally move their way eloquently through life saying "please", "thank you" and "excuse me/ pardon me". It is as if they are in a crowd of people and they gently make their way through by saying these kind words and they literally create a path through the crowd with their kindness. They get to where they want in life more efficiently and with much more pleasure by saying these words. They also make other people feel good along the way.

Millionaires of Kindness make sure they say their "pleases, thank yous and excuse mes" nearly every chance they get. Millionaires look for the opportunities in life to extend respect and kindness with these gentle words. They are able to move through life with humbleness, eloquence and kindness by saying please, thank you and excuse me/ pardon me at every chance they get.

Millionaires ask lots of questions and extend invitations. They give very little advice...rather they offer support

Millionaires of Kindness ask lots of questions. They want to hear about how another person is doing or what they are thinking. Millionaires are genuinely curious and caring. Questions and invitations are user-friendly and allow a Millionaire to move through life without forcing ideas and advice onto other people. This allows people to come to their own conclusions. If your way is the best and truest way, then others will agree when you invite their ideas and gently ask questions about them.

It could be as simple as:

"How are you doing?"

"Is there anything I can help you with?"

These are very kind questions, and most of the time,

people will respond to them constructively.

Millionaires also extend invitations. This is a way of asking a question without really asking a question. This is more of a statement that asks or allows another person to share something about themselves.

> "Tell me about that."

> "Just let me know if I can help you."

These are very kind ways of having a person open up and talk about their life without asking questions.

Sometimes a person doesn't feel like opening up. Perhaps a Millionaire has asked a question and the person doesn't want to talk. A Millionaire may respond with something such as:

> "I'm sorry I didn't mean to pry or get too personal.....

> ....just let me know if I can help you".

Millionaires make it easy for others to open up and share their feelings. They ask questions and extend gentle invitations. Then, most importantly, Millionaires listen.

Millionaires of Kindness use simple questions and invitations to make it very easy and comfortable for others to share their life with them. They sincerely care about others and like to hear other people's stories... from what is bothering them to what they feel good about. Millionaires understand how important it may be for another person to feel the freedom to talk about a problem or something that is bothering them and holding them back. They offer a gentle lift and inspiration to others by asking questions, extending invitations and listening with kindness and respect.

Millionaires say "I'm sorry I hurt you" when they offend or hurt someone

Millionaires of Kindness understand that even with their best intentions on being kind, occasionally they will hurt another person with their words or actions. They truly mean to be kind to others and sometimes they make a mistake or misunderstanding in communication and they inadvertently hurt another person.

Millionaires recognize when they hurt someone and they take action. They go out of their way to right a wrong. Millionaires begin the process of apologizing. Millionaires understand that apologizing and saying you're sorry is a process that takes some time...it is usually not just a single event.

When Millionaires do or say something that hurts somebody (hopefully this was inadvertent), they understand that it is going to take time and multiple attempts to right the wrong that they have done. Millionaires understand that it is going to take more than one attempt at saying "I'm sorry" and they state the reason why. For example:

"I'm sorry I said that...it was really rude of me"

"I'm sorry I can be a real jerk sometimes...I'm really sorry"

"I know I do that a lot, I'm sorry I hurt your feelings".

"I'm really sorry for all the times I've hurt you"

Often times people will hurt somebody and then say "I'm sorry" and expect that to solve the problem. Saying "I'm sorry" one time will only resolve some of the incidents where you have hurt someone.

Millionaires know that it is usually going to take more than one apology to resolve a mistake of hurting someone. This is because the hurt person may be in a reactionary mood and they are not in a position to fully resolve and forgive the person who has hurt them. It usually takes time.

An example of this is if you accidentally hit someone on the head with a hammer. When people get hit on the head, there is a tendency to react in anger, sometimes even pushing another person away. A hit to the head is a very sensitive event and there is usually a strong reactionary period following the hit, usually from a few seconds to a few minutes. Saying "I'm sorry" immediately following the "hit on the head" and during the reactionary period following is a nice and helpful gesture. It is also important to communicate the apology following the reactionary period when the person is calmed down and "back to being with it".

The above comparison also is comparable to everyday "hurts" in life. The human psyche is emotionally sensitive to hurtful words just as the head is physically sensitive to the hammer. Saying "I'm sorry" immediately upon realizing that you said or did something hurtful is important, as is apologizing "down the road" after the reactionary period.

Millionaires understand it is going to take an average of three apologies to resolve the hurt caused by unknowingly doing or saying something. These apologies may need to occur over a period of minutes, hours, days, weeks and even years to have their maximum effectiveness.

Whatever the situation, Millionaires of Kindness can instantly be humble and have the courage to say that they are sorry. They also know that they must persevere by saying "I'm sorry" multiple times and also stating what they are sorry for. Millionaires stick with it and over time their humbleness will win over the hearts of others that they may have hurt and even those who they haven't hurt.

Millionaires tell other People that they are "Right" when they are, and sometimes when they aren't "Right"

Millionaires of Kindness know that it feels really good inside when someone tells you that you are right about something. Millionaires understand that the "desire to be right" sometimes ranks right up there with thirst, hunger and sex in human desires. Sometimes, it can seem even more important.

Millionaires understand that they can bring out the best in other people easier through encouragement rather than discouragement. Telling another person they are right is one of the easiest and most effective ways to do this.

Millionaires know that most of our everyday conversations in life are not about critical life and death things. There are many ways we can interpret our observations, opinions, beliefs and events of our lives. In many cases, there isn't even a right or wrong way. Different people will see things in many different ways. Depending on the people that you interact with, there is a good chance that there will be some that feel that they must be right. A Millionaire could have the exact correct answer and there may be someone that will debate and battle them to the end of time.

Millionaires don't have the time or energy to get in a heated debate about sports, politics, religion, TV shows, Movie stars and the like. If someone gets extremely passionate about their side of the story, Millionaires simply let it go. They will say something like:

"You know, the more I think about it, you are right about that."

Most of the time, that statement will pretty much diffuse the tensions. Millionaires find themselves telling other people things like:

"Wow I never thought of it like that.... I think you are right".

"You know, you made me see things differently... thank you".

"Ya know, you're right about that".

"Man you got me on that...you were right about that".

Millionaires know they build very loyal relationships with the people that they tell that they are right about some things. Throughout their life, most people have probably been told that they were wrong much more often than they were told they were right. Millionaires see the pain in other people. When a person becomes so adamant that they are right about something, Millionaires see the deep pain in that person.

Millionaires feel that it is often more constructive to be "Kind" than to be "Right" in most of life's everyday conversations. Millionaires know they have a great opportunity to be kind and make someone's day just by saying "Your Right". It makes others happy and it feels great to be kind to others.

Millionaires know that there may be some challenges to telling others that they are right. The good thing is that the main challenge is within the Millionaire them self. There is pride and stubbornness. These are internal feelings within people. A Millionaire is pretty much in control of their destiny and in most everyday situations, they can look past their stubbornness and pride. All a Millionaire has to do is say "you're right". Sounds simple enough huh?

Millionaires of Kindness have the courage and humbleness to tell another person they are right about something when they are right. Millionaires have even more courage and humbleness to tell someone they are right when they know they aren't right. In most cases, Millionaires would rather be kind than to be right. Millionaires love to be kind to others by telling other people that they are right...when they are right and even sometimes when they aren't right.

Millionaires admit they are "Wrong" when they are, and sometimes when they know they aren't "Wrong"

Millionaires of Kindness don't get caught up into fighting trivial battles and losing valuable time and energy in having to be "right" all the time. They realize it is usually better to be kind than to be right. Most of the time!

Millionaires ask the question: "How does it feel when you know someone is wrong about something and they will just not admit it?" It can be very frustrating and you can end up in a battle that doesn't seem to have an end. Could it be easier and better for you to say that you are wrong (knowing you are right)?

And for that matter, maybe say you are wrong (when you know you are right)?

You may have to reread what I just said. It does make sense. Why be the pompous person that has to be right all the time when you can be the stronger person and be humble and say "I am wrong" without fear?

It could be something as trivial as to whom won the Super Bowl the previous year or it could be as foggy as to what happened 20 or 30 or more years ago. Come on, it is probably not a life and death situation. What does fighting over a trivial matter do for your personal growth? You could argue and argue even if you do know the facts about something rather trivial. If it is trivial and not life and death, why not just say: "You know, I think you are right about that, I'm wrong."

Be a Millionaire and be the bigger person and say you are wrong when you are wrong and sometimes say you're wrong when you aren't wrong. Most of the time it is better to be kind than to be right. Most of the time! Just say you are wrong a couple of times a day and watch your relationships improve.

If you are going to be wrong about something in life, make it be being wrong about you being wrong. I hope you get it and have fun!!!

Millionaires of Kindness are happy to admit they are wrong when they are wrong. They are also happy sometimes to say they are wrong when they know they are not wrong and when they know that it will make someone happy. Millionaires are aware of the value of making another person happy, rather than being stubborn and not able to say they are wrong about something.

Millionaires say "It hurts me when you (do something that hurts me)"

Millionaires of Kindness understand that when they have angry feelings towards another person, it is most likely that they feel hurt for some real or perceived action that someone said or did.

It is as simple as this. Millionaires understand and get this principle. They use this to their advantage in life, for it solves most of their problems they have with other people.

Millionaires recognize that hurt is a very delicate and powerful emotion. Millionaires will even go as far as to think that the wealth and Millions a person attains in their life is rather directly proportional to how well that they are able to understand the hurt in their own life and others. And then, how well they can resolve it constructively so that everyone involved feels better.

Hurt, like any other emotion, can be constructive or destructive in one's life. It is easy to think that hurt is bad and destructive. Sometimes people will believe that hurt is always bad and destructive and they have no choice but to accept the bad. Millionaires understand this as destructive thinking and they avoid this type of thinking.

Millionaires think constructively about hurt. They make the hurt they feel work to their benefit. They get to the cause of hurt and then they fix the hurt and make amends. Millionaires don't let hurt linger. They step up and confront the hurt, find out the cause and then make constructive changes and reparations.

Hurt can also include other feelings such as frustration, feelings of betrayal, feelings of being lied to, feeling that the person treats them as unequal, etc. Millionaires know what to do. They say the magic words to the person that has hurt them: "It hurts me when you _____. The blank could be anything that they do or say that hurts.

Millionaires understand that expression of anger and ill feelings are almost always destructive to relationships and to their own self. Yes, a Millionaire feels anger and ill feelings. They recognize that there is a deeper feeling and this is hurt. Millionaires understand that expression of anger and ill feelings is usually destructive. So Millionaires express their true feelings, which is the hurt that they feel.

Millionaires understand the challenge to expressing hurt to others is being perceived as weak, weird, and possibly many other things. Millionaires have the courage to open up their sensitivities and vulnerabilities to others. Many times others will laugh or make fun of a Millionaire's sensitivities. This is where Millionaires are truly strong. They realize that some people may not accept this openness right away. Sometimes other people will make fun of sensitivities and at many times it is going to take a series of "It hurts me when you _____," to help another person to communicate on a deeper and more sensitive level.

Millionaires are aware that some and even many people will not respond to the first "It hurts me when you _____." Millionaires are strong and understand that "persistence, persistence, persistence" sometimes necessary to make relationships work. They understand that they must say "It hurts me when you _____" many times before the person understands and "gets it".

Millionaires understand that saying that they are hurt when they are is one of the biggest keys to life and relationship building and being at peace inside. Millionaires also understand that many times when they say that they are hurt that it may seem like it falls on deaf ears. Other people may be stubborn and may not understand what a Millionaire is saying or means. They may laugh or stubbornly resist responding to a Millionaire's sharing their feelings of hurt. Millionaires understand that many people are not going to understand that they shared that they are hurt and they actually expect it. Many people just do not get this point so Millionaires persist and without reverting to anger or frustration, they once again state "It hurts me when you _____.".

Millionaires of Kindness are happy, wealthy and strong because they can identify when they are angry and they know that they are hurt. Millionaires are proactive in resolving their hurt simply by saying "I'm hurt" or "It hurts me when you _____". Millionaires do not lash out at others in hurt and

anger. They express their feelings calmly and objectively. Millionaires will express their feelings over and over until the other person understands. It is simple self-expression and does not use anger and other hurtful emotions.

Millionaires listen to others deeply and intently, without interruption. They also let others cry without interruption

Millionaires of Kindness understand that the majority of people want to be listened to without interruption or judgment. Most people want to be admired and adored for their ideas and feelings. Most people want to feel validated and at the center of attention and they don't want advice or to be told what to do.

Millionaires are so secure in themselves that they don't feel the need to talk a lot about themselves. They actually enjoy listening to others more than they like to talk about themselves. It actually fulfills the need to listen to others and to feel empathy for others. Millionaires actually learn a lot by listening to other people's life experiences and stories. Of course, there are those people that rub a

Millionaire the wrong way or will talk for hours and hours. Millionaires will find a respectful way to disengage from people who are destructive and draining, with minimal hurt to their feelings.

Millionaires simply sit back and listen. They are genuinely interested in other people's lives. They pay attention and go with the flow of another person's story. They ask questions and respectfully inquire deeper into the person's life when it feels right and is appropriate. Of course, if a Millionaire asks a question that makes the person uncomfortable, they will back off and apologize for being too intrusive. For example, a Millionaire might say,

"Oh I'm sorry to get too personal, I am just interested in your life"

Then they may say something like:

"Keep going...please don't be afraid to let me know if I ask you something that makes you feel uncomfortable"

Millionaires just keep in the flow. They don't have that many opportunities to ask something that makes the person feel uncomfortable because they are listening most of the time.

Millionaires understand the importance of another person's deep feelings. There are feelings such as deep sadness that transcend words. Millionaires know that when they do get the rare opportunity of another person opening up and crying in front of them, they know it is a sacred event and experience.

Millionaires let other people cry without interruption. They allow other people to have their sacred experience deep down inside, for however long it takes. It may be minutes or even hours. It may be for many periods over the course of time. Millionaires just let the person feel and get it out and they are honored to have that experience with another person.

This is one of the specific and most important ways that Millionaires listen to others. This can have an enormous impact on another person's life and Millionaires know it! And all that a Millionaire does is once again, to sit back and listen and support someone else.

Millionaires of Kindness understand that one of the easiest ways they can support, love and help another person, especially through difficult emotions, is to sit back and listen. Millionaires are careful not interrupt the sacred and tender experience of another person's expression of their emotions. Millionaires find themselves wealthy with love and kindness because they do not tell a person what to do, they simply listen with kindness.

Millionaires make Eye Contact with others often

Millionaires of Kindness look directly into other people's eyes with softness and kindness. They do so because they really do care about other people. Millionaires understand that this action communicates deep compassion and they do this with respect. Looking into another person's eyes is universal and does not require a common spoken language. It shows that you have the energy and excitement to care about them, and that makes people feel special.

Millionaires understand that some people will look away when someone looks into their eyes. Millionaires do not take it personally and they know it is usually shyness and unfamiliarity that cause some people to do this. Millionaires respect others feelings and do not make the person feel uncomfortable by being too persistent by looking into the person's eyes too often. They also do not make sexual eye contact or aggressive eye contact that make others feel uncomfortable. They take their time with compassion and build trust while not forcing eye contact.

Millionaires look into another person's eyes with compassion, it is an act of kindness. People from all cultures, continents and places all over Earth recognize the intimacy and trust of eye contact. People from all over the globe can relate to one another by looking into other people's eyes. A genuine, soft meeting of the eyes does incredible things to a person. Millionaires get to experience this everyday as they genuinely look into other people's eyes with compassion and really light them up. They make others feel great and move them to do their very best in their life.

Millionaires understand that gentle, caring eye contact is one of the easiest ways to extend kindness to others. Millionaires literally soften other people's souls just through a few moments of eye contact. Once again, Millionaires don't tell others what to do or how to do something, they simply give kindness through soft eye contact.

Millionaires Smile Often

Millionaires of Kindness understand that smiles are universal. Smiles make constructive things happen in life. They know that smiles give them power with themselves and with other people. It feels great to smile. A smile allows the release of happy chemicals in the brain and they flood throughout the body. Millionaires know that smiles are a great way to begin and build relationships.

Smiles are a way of giving and sharing kindness. Smiles cause a surge in happy chemicals flooding a person's brain. Millionaires smile by themselves when no one else can see and they smile with other people. Millionaires smile at others. They remain smiling with others even when the smiles are not returned. One thing that you can count on is that Millionaires smile!!!!

Millionaires connect their smiles with their other expressions of their true and deep kindness. It is the eye contact, the compliments, the caring, and the listening.

Millionaires let their soul and deepest kindness shine-through their smile.

Millionaires know that smiles are contagious. Once smiles reach a certain energy amongst people, they can and do spread like wildfire. Millionaires find that their life is in such a happy groove when they are smiling that life is truly magical. They are in command of this magical world that feeds off of smiles. Kindness is everywhere and Millionaires orchestrate it all.

Millionaires of Kindness understand the power of the genuine smile. They naturally combine their smile with their other expressions of kindness. Millionaires light up the room with that special smile and soon after it seems everyone is smiling and kindness A single person has the power to life the emotions of many, and Millionaires sure know how to do it.... with eye contact, with kindness and with that irresistible SMILE.

Millionaires give Complements to others all day long

Millionaires of Kindness feel great when they give complements. They also know they make other people feel great when to receive complements. Complements sure do make the world go around.

Millionaires give complements without expectation of anything in return. They give complements because they recognize other people doing good things and they want to be kind to others and tell them. Millionaires want others to feel great inside and want to help them to reach excellence and do and be their very best.

Millionaires are full of complements and appreciation of others and they spend complements lavishly. Millionaires walk through life and leave a trail of happiness and people feeling good behind them because it is a beautiful thing to do and a beautiful way to live life.

Millionaires are very kind and respectful when giving their complements. Millionaires are extra careful in the area of sexual related complements. Sexual related complements to someone other than your sexual partner can be a very sensitive area, where well intentioned compliments can interpreted in a hurtful or disrespecting way. Millionaires are aware of this and are very careful when giving sexual related complements.

Millionaires follow this general test for sexual related complements. They should be able to say the complement in front of a long list of both parties' friends and family, husbands and wives, and even in a public forum. If it passes this test, then it is probably an appropriate complement. If it doesn't, it is probably an inappropriate complement and they shouldn't say it. There are so many ways to complement others and help them to feel fantastic that Millionaires usually avoid the potential complications of sexual compliments and stick to ones that complement the person.

Here are some examples of some Kind and Respectful Complements:

1. You look very nice today.

2. I appreciate how you make me feel good when I see you.

3. It is always great to see you.

4. You must be very proud of your son, he is such a great person.

5. You are always making me smile.

6. You're the best.

7. You did an awesome job on the house.

8. I really admire you.

Millionaires recognize the simplicity of giving complements. They know that genuine complements are constructive.

Millionaires also recognize what destructive thought processes get in the way of giving compliments freely. A person can start believing that another person doesn't deserve complements for a number of reasons. These can be:

1. The person has already been complemented on the task or achievement.

2. The task or achievement has been done by lots of others already.

3. The fear that if the person is complemented that they might not continue to do the task or achievement.

4. That they are being too nice and that it is "not real" to give complements.

Millionaires are aware of these limitations and they not only work through them, they blast right past the destructive thoughts if they are limiting the amount of compliments that they are giving out.

Millionaires of Kindness give out complements all day long. Complements flow naturally for the Millionaire. They understand that the kindness of complements will bring out the best in others. Millionaires "are over" the limitations that restrict complements...mostly that they are being too nice and that it is not real. Millionaires do not let

destructive thoughts of criticism, or giving no complements, get in the way of a genuine life of constructive complements.

Millionaires receive Compliments with acceptance and gratitude

Millionaires of Kindness understand that just as much as giving compliments is a kind and generous thing to do, receiving compliments can be a very kind and overlooked way to express kindness. Millionaires receive many complements throughout most days. They do so because they are very kind to other people and very often people will compliment them. Millionaires are gracious when accepting a compliment, much the same way they are when accepting a thank you.

Millionaires will first acknowledge the compliment. This may be as simple as with a thank you. It is nice to directly thank the specific compliment. For example: "Thank you for saying my hair looks nice". "Thank you for the compliment". "That makes me feel good...thank you".

Millionaires take time to absorb the compliment... to take-it-all-in... to humbly celebrate the compliment for a few moments. Accepting the compliment is honoring and being kind to the giver of the compliment.

Millionaires will take a few seconds (perhaps approximately five to ten seconds) to accept a compliment. This is a beautiful way to acknowledge the person who compliments. This is a way of soaking in the well-deserved compliment (heck, it's perfectly alright to feel good about yourself).

A Millionaire's response to a complement may be something like:

1. Oh wow, thank you so much for the complement.

2. It feels so great to be appreciated by you.

3. Thank you for making me feel so special.

4. Wow...you really made my day. Thank you.

Millionaires break the daily routine and literally "stop time" to accept a complement. The one thing Millionaires are careful of is feeling obligated to return a complement. Although at first thought it may seem like it is the "right thing to do" by returning a complement, perhaps it is healthy and constructive not to return it so fast. Returning a complement relatively immediately following the receiving of a complement may, in fact, overshadow the complement itself. Millionaires sometimes let the complement absorb in. Also, the person giving the complement will feel recognized for their giving of a complement.

Millionaires enjoy receiving complements and recognize that the acceptance of a complement can be a complement in itself.

How a Millionaire of Kindness responds to a complement is up for interpretation and has been chosen based on years of experience and instinct. There are times where it is great to return a complement and there are times when it is awesome to accept a complement and enjoy and treasure it. Millionaires resist the pressure to return a compliment, at least immediately. Millionaires understand that it is not necessarily a bad thing to accept a complement and see where that takes the conversation and the relationship.

Millionaires tell others that they are "Proud" of them often

Millionaires of Kindness understand that the feeling of pride is one of the most powerful, if not the most powerful of human emotions. Millionaires live in a world that is swelling with pride. Success and kindness comes easy when you are feeling genuine pride. This pride is not to be confused with the pride of being a "tough guy" or false pride.

Millionaires define pride as the feeling of the deepest respect and appreciation of yourself and your fellow human being without judgment, or most importantly, competition. There is no comparison or competition with pride. This makes it possible to be proud of anybody for anything.

There seems to be an unwritten social definition of pride that says you must be the very best for others to be proud of you. Pride is reserved only for the richest and for the people who have achieved more than another person. The average great person who is excellent, but not a CEO, Movie star, Rock star etc. usually get shorted on receiving Pride.

Unfortunately, by using this limited social definition, there are many people that don't know what true pride feels like. This can be a very empty place to be. Somehow, a person must realize that they can feel pride even though they have no idea what they could possibly feel like.

In a Millionaires world, Pride is available for everyone to feel for each other. They have an abundance of Pride. This Pride seems to just keep flowing out in nearly everything they do. Most Millionaires weren't born with this perfect feeling of pride. They had to learn it as they went through life. They realize that life is easier, more fulfilling and feels better when they are feeling pride.

Millionaires tell others that they are proud of them and they also tell themselves the same thing. It is as simple as:

"I'm proud of you"

"Wow...you did great work, I'm really proud of you."

"I'm always so proud of you, I know you are going to be successful."

Millionaires observe that it can be difficult for many people to say "I'm proud of you" to another person. It can sound and feel uncomfortable. The chances are the reason is that they have not received much appreciation and another person feeling proud of them. This is the unfortunate effect of a shortage of pride.

The great thing is that pride is a limitless natural

resource in the world. It is unlike gold, silver, oil and other limited resources. Millionaires simply decide to be proud of themselves and others. Pride is right there in front of everyone and there is more than you can ever use. It is limitless. It may feel awkward at first. It is because it is new. Millionaires have jumped right in sharing pride and have never stopped being proud of themselves and others.

Millionaires of Kindness become Millionaires because they know how to find their way through a situation where they don't know exactly where they are going. They know "there is a million bucks out there" even when they can't see it in the moment. Millionaires have the uncanny knack of how to get there...they have the patience to figure out how to get there. Millionaires just jump into life and begin spending kindness and giving and receiving pride in lavish amounts. It all starts by telling one person you are proud of them and it builds and builds. All of a sudden you are genuinely proud of yourself and proud of many others. Life is grand.

A Few More Important Words...

Thank you for allowing a part of me into your life. I hope that you are inspired to go out and spend Millions of Dollars in Kindness. It is really as simple as that. You have my permission to be greedy and selfish. Go out and spend, spend, spend! Have fun and make others feel special...and make yourself into a Millionaire of Kindness!

In summary: Don't say "but, however and yet". Careful using those "all or nothing" words...better to use those "in-between words. When someone says "Thank You" say "You're Welcome". Make sure you say "Please, Thank You" and "Pardon/Excuse Me" in large amounts.

Ask lots of questions and extend invitations to others. Offer support for others and give very little advice. Say "I'm sorry I hurt you" when you hurt someone and give the reason why. Then say it later a few more times. Tell others they are "Right" when they are right about something and also tell them they are "Right" sometimes when they are not right.

Say you are "Wrong" about something when you are wrong, and also sometimes when you aren't wrong. Say "It hurts me" when someone hurts you. Tell them why. Be prepared for them not to hear it and be prepared to say it again. Listen to others when they are talking to you...let them talk themselves out...don't interrupt them. Also don't interrupt others when they are crying...let them cry it all out. Enjoy the experience with them. Don't give unsolicited advice.

Smile and make eye contact with others. Look people right into their eyes and don't be afraid to look deeply into their eyes...be genuine and don't be too weird about it. Give compliments all day long to others. Accept compliments with elegance and grace. Stop and appreciate the moment and the person giving you the compliment.

Maybe most importantly, tell others you are Proud of them, especially for the little things. There is such a shortage of Pride in many people's hearts. As a Millionaire, kick start the Kindness Economy and tell others you and others are Proud of them.

It's easy. Spend, spend, and spend, the kindness you have inside of you!

Peter

Endnote

Dr. Peter T. Zrinscak D.C. has spent years traveling and associating with all walks of life. He has a Bachelor's Degree in Chemical Engineering from New Mexico State University and earned his Doctor of Chiropractic from New York Chiropractic College in his young life. He is an avid outdoorsman and survivalist, and enjoys the company of many. He is a beloved friend to those that know him and published this book to pass-on some of the lessons in communication he has learned over the last few decades.

Be kind to each other, and you will have millions awaiting you in the world now, and in the world to come. In the words of Jesus, lay up your treasures in heaven.

God Bless!

Title: Be a Millionaire of Kindness
Website: www.billionaireofkindness.com
Publisher: Hamilton Enterprises, Denver Colorado
Date Published: August 4, 2015
Copyrighted: August 4, 2015©
Author: Dr. Peter Zrinscak D.C.
Contributor: David G. Hamilton, MBA
ISBN: 978-0988769496
Printed by Create Space Publishing, a subsidiary or Amazon